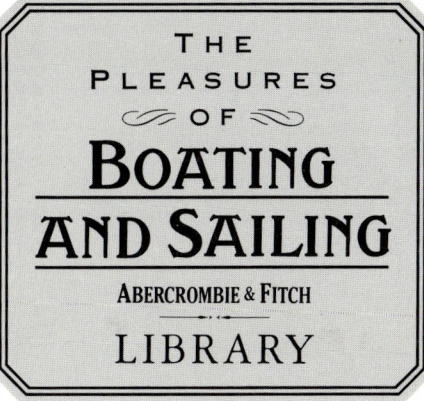

BOOKSELLERS
EST. 1892

Introduction

An island race has always held a fascination for water, and none more so than the British, whose early history of seafaring in no small way helped shape the map and destiny of the world in which we live today.

On a smaller scale, however, we have always liked to mess about in boats, no matter what size or form. For the purposes of this small volume, we have limited ourselves to unmotorised transport, whether on inland waterways or the waters surrounding "this sceptred isle".

There was a great vogue in Victorian times for boating parties, as the tradition of the Regatta was established. Henley was the best and initially most exclusive of these, where spectators would mingle on meadows leading to the Thames, in a seemingly endless flow of champagne and strawberries, picnics and parties. The actual water sports consisted of fierce rowing competitions between teams of fit young men from the top public schools, or from the colleges of Oxford and Cambridge universities. This became firmly established as a date in the social season, not entirely for the sport on the river.

A more leisurely tradition for punting or rowing on the rivers evolved out of this, taking hampers for waterside picnics, making small expeditions, generally enjoying the delights of the riverbank which often proved a most romantic setting.

As Henley was a beacon to start the English Season, so Cowes Week traditionally ended it, before everyone took off for the summer, which they would usually spend on their estates in Scotland before it became fashionable to take villas abroad. There the same people could gather on the lawns of the Royal Yacht Squadron or Royal London Yacht Club (essential, of course, to belong to the right club in this as any other sport) partially to socialise and partially to watch the spectacle of yachts competing on the waters of the Solent. The rules for the racing were, and still are, governed

by the Royal Yacht Squadron, and as yacht design has developed more and more streamlined craft, the racing proves ever more dramatic both for participant and spectator. Competition from across the Atlantic in the form of the yacht '*America*' in the late nineteenth century, had considerable influence over these future developments. The two countries' wealthiest magnates would race each other for the much coveted America's Cup continually refining and redesigning ocean-going yachts to the sophisticated models we have today.

As a small compilation of the wealth of writings about those nostalgic days, the following gives some impression of timeless pleasures to be gained from being on water, with the sun and wind in your face.

Jenny de Gex, 1991

On Inland Waterways

Every one who has been upon a walking or a boating tour, living in the open air, with the body in constant exercise and the mind in fallow, knows true ease and quiet. The irritating action of the brain is set at rest; we think in a plain, unfeverish temper; little things seem big enough, and great things no longer portentous; and the world is smilingly accepted as it is.

The Pocket RLS, Robert Louis Stevenson, 1907

THE RIVER BANK

'This has been a wonderful day!' said he, as the Rat shoved off and took to the sculls again. 'Do you know, I've never been in a boat before in all my life.'

'What?' cried the Rat, open-mouthed. 'Never been in a – you never – well, I – what have you been doing, then?'

'Is it so nice as all that?' asked the Mole shyly, though he was quite prepared to believe it as he leant back in his seat and surveyed the cushions, the oars, the rowlocks, and all the fascinating fittings, and felt the boat sway lightly under him.

'Nice? It's the *only* thing,' said the Water Rat solemnly, as he leant forward for his stroke. 'Believe me, my young friend, there is *nothing* – absolutely nothing – half so much worth doing as simply messing about in boats. Simply messing,' he went on dreamily: 'messing–about–in–boats; messing –'

'Look ahead, Rat!' cried the Mole suddenly.

It was too late. The boat struck the bank full tilt. The dreamer, the joyous oarsman, lay on his back at the bottom of the boat, his heels in the air.

'– about in boats – or *with* boats,' the Rat went on composedly, picking himself up with a pleasant laugh. 'In or out of 'em, it doesn't matter. Nothing seems really to matter, that's the charm of it.'

The Wind in the Willows, Kenneth Grahame, 1908

Angling Scenery

The meadows were still uncleared of hay when she and Con rowed downstream that afternoon and the air was thick with the scent of it. Lying in the boat, sleepy, she heard a kingfisher travel past with a thin high scream that was like the long fading scratch of a pencil on a slate. The sun was hot on her face as she lay on the cushions and presently Con leaned forward and covered her face with a big clean handkerchief.

'You'll get sick, lying there in the sun.'

'I'm asleep already,' she said.

Some time later he said, 'Man a-fishing', and through her thick sleepiness she heard him call:

'Any luck?'

'Not a touch.'

'Too bright, I expect,' Con said. 'Too hot. They'll bite about seven. What are you using?'

The Feast of July, H. E. Bates, 1954

Watermanship

Watermanship, as a technical term, may be said to consist in adapting oneself to circumstances and exigencies during the progress of a boat. A good waterman keeps time with facility, a bad one only after much painstaking – if at all. A good waterman adapts himself to every roll of the boat, sits tight to his seat, anticipates an incipient roll, and rights the craft so far as he can by altering his centre of gravity while yet plying his oar. A bad waterman is more or less helpless when a boat is off its keel, or when he encounters rough water. So long as the boat is level, he may be able to do even more work than the good waterman, but when the boat rolls he cannot help himself, still less can he right the ship and so help others to work, as can the good waterman.

Good watermen can jump into a racing boat and sit her off-hand; bad watermen will be unsteady in a keelless boat even after days of practice.

One or two good watermen are the making of a crew, especially when time is short for practice. They will raise the standard of rowing of all their colleagues, simply by keeping the balance of the boat.

Rowing, R. P. P. Rowe and C. M. Ritman, 1903

EIGHTS

The enormous eight young men in the thread-like skiff – the skiff that would scarce have seemed an adequate vehicle for the tiny 'cox' who sat facing them – were staring up at Zuleika with that uniformity of impulse which, in another direction, had enabled them to bump a boat on two of the previous 'nights'. If tonight they bumped the next boat, Univ., then would Judas be three places 'up' on the river; and tomorrow Judas would have a Bump Supper. Furthermore, if Univ. were bumped tonight, Magdalen might be bumped tomorrow. Then would Judas, for the first time in history, be head of the river. Oh tremulous hope! Yet, for the moment, these eight young men seemed to have forgotten the awful responsibility that rested on their over-developed shoulders. Their hearts, already strained by rowing, had been transfixed this afternoon by Eros' darts. All of them had seen Zuleika as she came down to the river; and now they sat gaping up at her, fumbling with their oars. The tiny cox gaped too; but he it was who first recalled duty. With piping adjurations he brought the giants back to their senses. The boat moved away down stream, with a fairly steady stroke.

Not in a day can the traditions of Oxford be sent spinning. From all the barges the usual punt-loads of young men were being ferried across to the towing-path – young men naked of knee, armed with rattles, post-horns, motor-hooters, gongs, and other instruments of clangour. Though Zuleika filled their thoughts, they hurried along the towing-path, as by custom, to the starting-point.

Zuleika Dobson, Max Beerbohm, 1911

Henley, Past and Future

The inauguration of a new era in the history of Henley Regatta naturally tends to make the mind wander into vistas of the past, perhaps even more than into speculations of the future. There are oarsmen living who can recollect when Henley Regatta did not even exist, and yet we are within an appreciable distance (three years) of the 'jubilee' of the gathering. There are sundry old Blues of the 1829 match still hale and hearty, and the regatta was not founded until ten years after that date. *Apropos* of that 1829 match, we have never seen it officially recorded that in the race Cambridge steered up the Bucks and Oxford in the Berks channel of the river, where the island divides it. Yet we have heard the Rev. T. Staniforth, the Oxford stroke, relate the fact. For some strange reason, the general opinion of *habitués* of the river prior to that match was that the Bucks channel gave the better course. The boughs of the island trees obstructed the Berks channel more than now, and this may explain the delusion. However, the Oxonians doubted the soundness of local opinion, and tested in practice the advantages of the two channels by timing themselves through each. They naturally found the inside course the shorter cut. In the race they adopted it, while Cambridge, so we hear, took the outside channel; and the previous lead of Oxford was more than trebled by the time that the boats came again into the main river.

Boating, W. D. Woodgate, 1889

Henley Regatta

The River Party

This is one of the most appreciated forms of hospitality in the summer-time that a bachelor can give. The form it takes is a question of his means. But people enjoy an outing on the river in a rowing-boat as much as a run in a motor-launch, which costs as many pounds as the boat does shillings. Men of quite small means can give a most pleasant day or afternoon on the river to those whose hospitality they have enjoyed. Of course the host must be a good rower, as should also be any other men he asks, especially if the party is to fill more than one boat.

The Book of Etiquette, Lady Troubridge, 1926

Punts and Poles

The popularity of punting is of comparatively recent date; forty years ago one might have rowed from Oxford to Putney and seen no punts but those containing fishermen. A few private pleasure-punts were built about thirty years since, but it is more particularly during the last ten years that their number has so greatly increased. It will not therefore be thought surprising that the present volume should contain a section devoted to this subject.

When boating for pleasure a punt possesses many advantages. The punter faces the direction in which the craft is travelling, and he or she can have a good view of the scenery; the position for punting is less cramped than that for rowing, and the stroke is more varied; the sitters can be more at ease than in a skiff, which must always be properly 'trimmed'. The punt is also better adapted for luncheon and tea, which is a great convenience on a journey, and obviates the necessity of reaching an hotel at any special time. As it travels much slower than a skiff more time must be allowed for any given distance, but twelve or fifteen miles down stream can easily be covered in a day by a good punter with one or two sitters. When the water is deep, or the bottom of the river soft, it is often quicker and less exertion to paddle the punt with a canoe paddle.

Boating, W. D. Woodgate, 1889

Meeting Other Boats

Between Iffley and Oxford is the most difficult bit of the river I know. You want to be born on that bit of water, to understand it. I have been over it a fairish number of times, but I have never been able to get the hang of it. The man who could row a straight course from Oxford to Iffley ought to be able to live comfortably, under one roof, with his wife, his mother-in-law, his eldest sister, and the old servant who was in the family when he was a baby.

First the current drives you on to the right bank, and then on to the left, then it takes you out into the middle, turns you round three times, and carries you up stream again, and always ends by trying to smash you up against a college barge.

Of course, as a consequence of this, we got in the way of a good many other boats, during the mile, and they in ours, and, of course, as a consequence of that, a good deal of bad language occurred.

Three Men in a Boat, J. K. Jerome, 1898

Eton Boating Song

Jolly boating weather,
And a hay harvest breeze,
Blade on the feather,
Shade off the trees,
Swing, swing together,
With your backs between your knees.

Skirting past the rushes,
Ruffling o'er the weeds,
Where the lock-stream gushes,
Where the cygnet feeds,
Let us see how the wine-glass flushes
At supper on Boveney meads.

Harrow may be more clever,
Rugby may make more row,
But we'll row, row for ever,
Steady from stroke to bow,
And nothing in life shall sever
The chain that is round us now.

Others will fill our places,
Dressed in the old light blue,
We'll recollect our races,
We'll to the flag be true,
And youth will be still in our faces
When we cheer for an Eton crew.

Twenty years hence this weather
May tempt us from office stools,
We may be slow on the feather,
And seem to the boys old fools,
But we'll still swing together
And swear by the best of schools.

Captain Algernon Heneage Drummond, 1865

ETON REGATTA

The Varsity Boat Race

Then again the Trial Eights will be going out in the Autumn, and our freshman begins to nourish a secret hope that if he shows up well in the races he may get a place in one of them, after which – who knows? In his heart of hearts he thinks that worse men have rowed at Putney. And to the dizziness of that ambition we may leave him, standing cheerfully, even with exultation, upon the threshold of a three years' slavery.

No other sport is so severe a mistress. Even the runner, for all the strictness of training which his ambition entails, enjoys an easier fame.

Cambridge Within, Charles Tennyson, 1913

THE OPEN SEA

White as a white sail on a dusky sea,
    When half the horizon's clouded and half free,
Fluttering between the dun wave and the sky,
Is hope's last gleam in man's extremity.
Her anchor parts! but still her snowy sail
Attracts our eye amidst the rudest gale:
Though every wave she climbs divides us more,
The heart still follows from the loneliest shore.

The Island, Fourth Canto, Lord Byron, 1823

A Tall Ship

"All I ask is a tall ship and a star to steer by,
 And a laughing yarn from a merry fellow rover,
And a quiet sleep and a sweet dream when the long trick's over."

John Masefield

A VERY YOUNG MARINER.

Queen Victoria's Yachting Excursion

*On Board the Victoria and Albert, Off St. Heliers, Jersey,
Wednesday, September 2, 1846.*

At a quarter-past seven o'clock we set off with Vicky, Bertie, Lady Jocelyn, Miss Kerr, Mdlle. Gruner, Lord Spencer, Lord Palmerston, and Sir James Clark (Mr. Anson and Colonel Grey being on board the "Black Eagle"), and embarked at *Osborne Pier*. There was a good deal of swell. It was fine, but very cold at first. At twelve we saw *Alderney*, and between two and three got into the *Alderney Race*, where there was a great deal of rolling, but not for long. We passed between *Alderney* and the French coast – *Cape de la Hague* – and saw the other side of *Alderney*; and then, later, *Sark*, *Guernsey*, and the other islands. After passing the *Alderney Race* it became quite smooth; and then Bertie put on his sailor's dress, which was beautifully made by the man on board who makes for our sailors. When he appeared, the officers and sailors, who were all assembled on deck to see him, cheered, and seemed delighted with him.

Leaves from a Journal of Our Life in the Scottish Highlands, and Yacht Excursions,
Queen Victoria, 1868

THE LIGHTHOUSE

The rocky ledge runs far into the sea,
    And on its outer point, some miles away,
The lighthouse lifts its massive masonry,
    A pillar of fire by night, of cloud by day.

And the great ships sail outward and return.
    Bending and bowing o'er the billowy swells,
And ever joyful, as they see it burn,
    They wave their silent welcomes and farewells.

They come forth from the darkness, and their sails
    Gleam for a moment only in the blaze,
And eager faces, as the light unveils,
    Gaze at the tower, and vanish while they gaze.

The mariner remembers when a child,
    On his first voyage, he saw it fade and sink;
And when, returning from adventures wild,
    He saw it rise again o'er ocean's brink.

                        H. W. Longfellow, 1865

A YOUNG MARINER.

Sacred Cowes

'Following the lead of the Prince of Wales, social England converted the regatta week at Cowes into one of the greatest social functions of the fashionable year. Society decreed that before it spread itself over Europe in the autumn its first taste of fresh air after the fatigues of the London season should be inhaled at the little town on the Solent . . .

'It was said of such gatherings, which were content to find accommodation in exiguous yachts' cabins and in single bedrooms at exorbitant rents in the narrow streets, that for seven days you belonged to one large family of the nicest and prettiest people in England. You idled under their balconies at all hours of the day and night, dined with them when you were hungry, sailed with them when you were nautical, flirted with them when you were amorous . . . The society was the same year after year. The same party crowded into the same little houses and filled the same villas; the same wicker chairs were set out on the club lawn and filled with identically the same people who had been pillars of the little town for years. Here they greeted each other almost like relations; here they are kindly, considerate, almost affectionate, and the outsider feels as an intruder upon a family party. They all know each other's little histories and secrets, and their conversations bristle with little allusions, the unintelligibility of which to all outside intelligence makes a high and inseparable barrier to all intercourse of the same kind . . .

Anon, 1887

Cowes Regatta

The Excitement of the Race

Then there is all the tense excitement of the closely·sailed race against great yachts of equal power and speed. Those moments when close-hauled, one stands at the wheel, all the crew lying flat along the weather deck watching one's every move, speculating as to one's judgment, as the two yachts draw nearer and nearer together. Hold on or come about? Tack under her lee, giving her a lee bow, or cross her? Such decisions have to be instantly made if races are to be won. The weather mark is just ahead. A rolling, tolling bell-buoy, plunging in the tideway. One must pass within a mere foot of it. Then it's up helm, away mainsheet and our spinnaker, as the water pours across the deck, cascading out of the scuppers, and off to the leeward mark with the huge spinnaker billowing out over the bow ... No; there is nothing quite so exciting – at least not for me.

Sacred Cowes, Anthony Heckstall-Smith, 1965

AN ANCIENT MARINER.

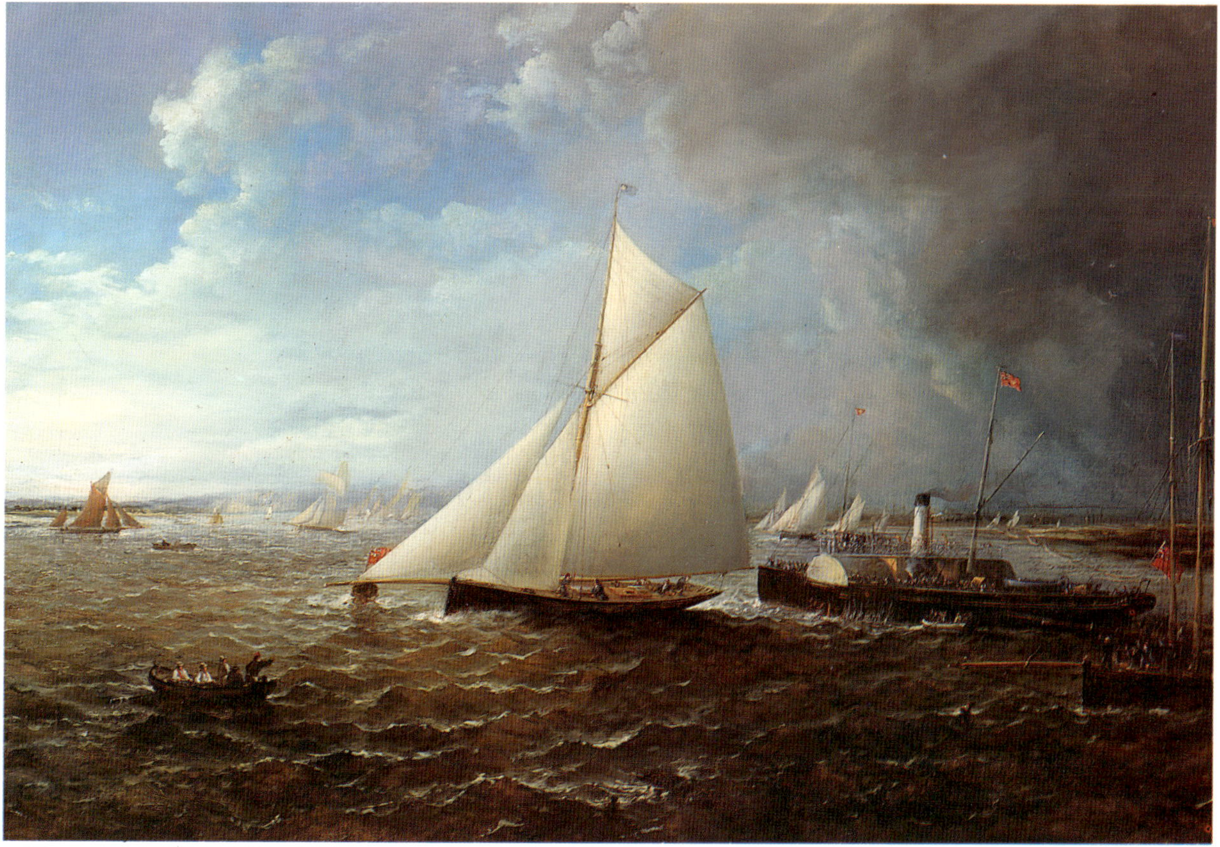

THE THRILL OF SAILING

I have sailed many kinds of craft; dinghies, ocean racers, skimming dishes and tubby cruisers. I have travelled fast on land, sea and in the air. I have raced on skis and down bob-runs and in ice-yachts. But I have never experienced the same thrill and sense of power as when sailing a first-class cutter in a fresh wind. It is well-nigh impossible to put into words the exhilaration one feels as one stands on the sloping deck, the wheel straining in one's hands, the great sweep of the mainsail towering above one, the blocks of the mainsheet making their own peculiar creaking noise over one's shoulder. The salt spray and spindrift flying upwards from the lee shrouds and the plunging stem that seems an infinite distance away. All the tremendous power of the hard pressed hull, the great lead keel below weighing hundreds of tons, and the thousands of square feet of straining canvas aloft, is in one's hands as they grip the wheel pulling and wrenching at every muscle in one's body. And through that wheel, the trembling nerves of the great vessel vibrate to one's fingers on the spokes. The slightest variation in the wind's force is instantly communicated to one, so that the yacht becomes a living creature to be driven just so hard but not one degree harder lest, with a crack like a rifle shot, a cleat is torn from the deck or a rigging screw breaks and in a crash of splintering wood, flailing wires and rending canvas, the mast goes over the side.

Sacred Cowes, Anthony Heckstall-Smith, 1965

WESTWARD, 1911

A King on Board

For a number of years we had a very good client, a man whose name was exceedingly well known in the City. He took a cruise in his yacht to Santander. Whilst lying in the harbour an equerry from the King of Spain came aboard and said the King would like to visit the yacht. The next afternoon the King came alongside in a launch. The skipper of the yacht was waiting for him at the top of the gangway with the owner in the background.

The King jumped up the companion ladder and shaking hands with the skipper he said:

"Have you got a whisky-and-soda aboard, Captain?"

The King admired the beautifully bright varnished deck fittings and bulwarks. "The best kept of any yacht I have ever seen." The skipper asked him if he would accept a gallon of the varnish; this the King did.

The King took tea aboard the yacht with the owner and his wife, and on leaving took the varnish away with him.

Sixty Years of Yachts, Herbert E. Julyan, 1950

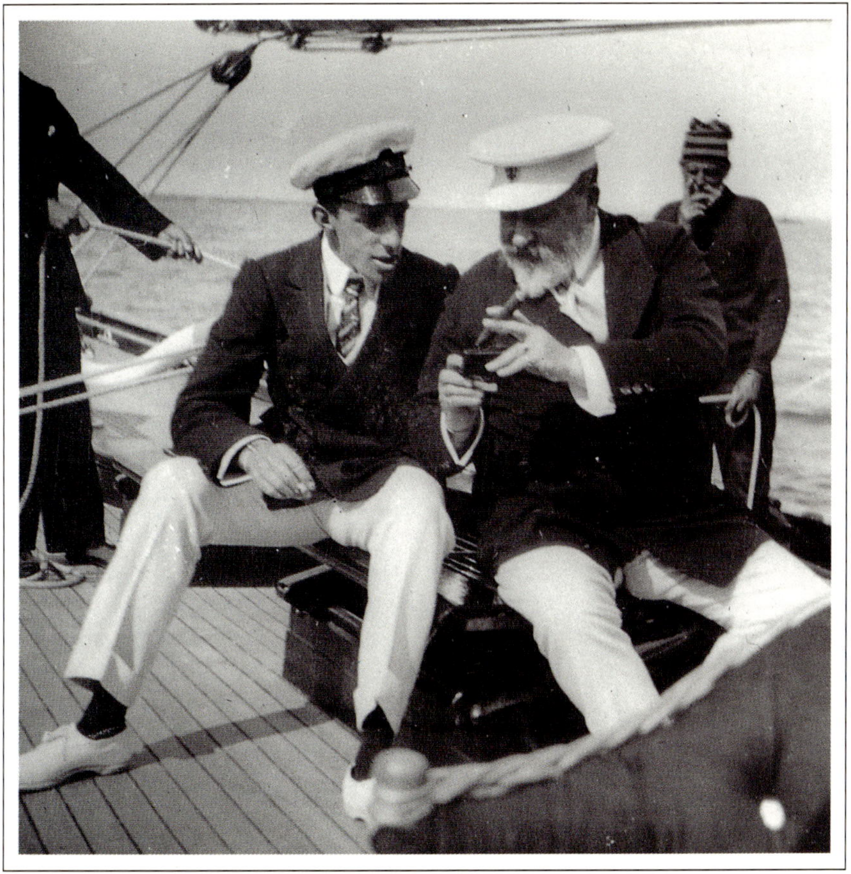

Affairs of State and Sea

I suppose no man loved the sea more than George V, yet it always seemed to me one of the onerous aspects of his calling that he was able to give so little time to sailing. I do not believe he was ever more happy than when racing aboard *Britannia* with a party of friends. Then for a few brief hours he could forget the affairs of state, the formalities of the court and put aside the burden of his office, and become merely the owner of a first-class racing cutter. He could haul on the mainsheet with his men or feel the kick of the rudder as he stood at the wheel, his blue eyes watching the leech of the jib, as he worked *Britannia* out to windward of her rivals. At such moments the King seemed to grow younger. Nonetheless, as soon as the race was over, he would return to the *Victoria and Albert* once more to attend to official business, the signing of state papers, the reading of telegrams and dispatches and the receiving of official guests. Other owners were free to talk over the day's racing in the cabins of their yachts, to put up their feet on the saloon settee and relax. But not *Britannia's* owner. At best, he could hope to snatch a couple of weeks' racing aboard his yacht in a whole season.

Sacred Cowes, Anthony Heckstall-Smith, 1965

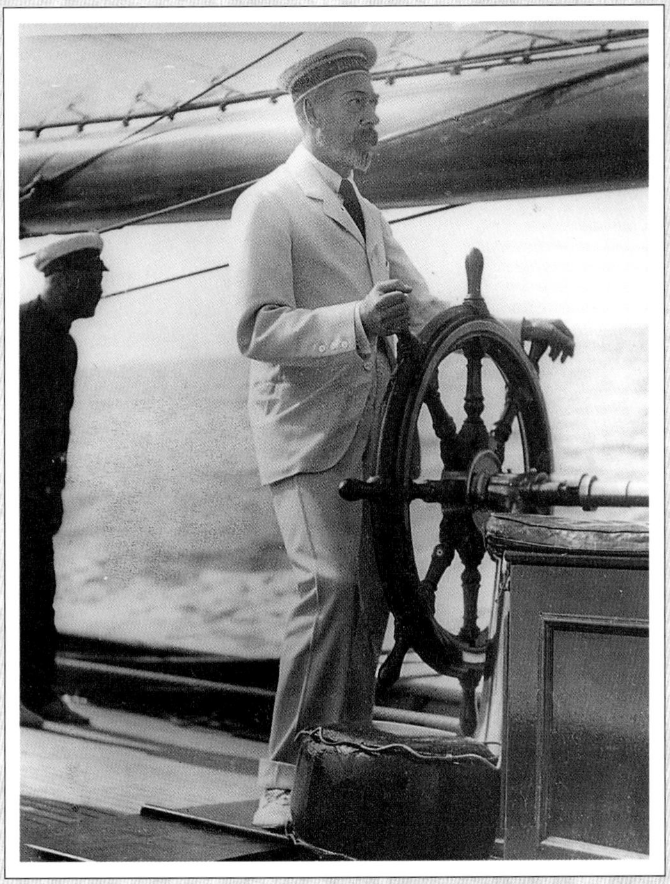

The Old Britannia

'We shall be for it before the day's out,' I said to Phil.

And for it we certainly were!

Soon after we came on a wind, a few seconds ahead of *Shamrock*, Phil was calling for the sheets to be eased as *Britannia* was beginning to wallow. The third leg of the course gave us a reach, with the wind a little for'ard of the beam, into the starting line. Now *Britannia* heeled to a tremendous angle with the water up the companion deck house. Phil, waist deep in water, was having difficulty steering her. Blinded by driving spray, he shouted to the second mate to give him a hand at the wheel, and called for a lashing to be tied round his waist to keep him from being swept overboard. We were travelling at fourteen knots and under the press of her whole mainsail and in the savage gusts of wind that crashed down from the high cliffs, the old yacht was practically unmanageable. Her entire lee deck was under water and her mainboom, with the sheet eased, but a few inches from the water. In a cloud of flying spray, we tore through the pleasure boats . . . .

'She won't bear up!' Phil shouted as he and the second mate forced the wheel over, the pair of them half buried in foam.

Then, with a crack, the clew of the jib carried away, mercifully easing the sorely pressed ship.

Now, our nearest rival, *Shamrock*, was minutes astern of us, so, in the gale and rising sea, Phil refrained from taking any chances and did not even set the spinnaker off the wind. Now, too, *Velsheda* and *Astra* had retired from the race; the latter having carried away most of the hanks on her mainsail.

Soon after we rounded the weather mark more than five minutes ahead of *Shamrock*, which was lying over almost on her beam ends, I saw her mast go over the side with a mighty splash.

So the old *Britannia* was the only one left in the race.

Sacred Cowes, Anthony Heckstall-Smith, 1965

BRITANNIA, 1924

The America

It has been stated that the *America* did not fairly win the cup now called the America Cup, for which many contests have since been fought. Few people really know how the first race for this cup was sailed. The facts are these. The *America* schooner had crossed from the States to Cowes to race against our British yachts in 1851. At the Cowes Regatta there was no cup which the *America* could compete for. She was not entitled to compete for a Queen's Cup. In order to test what she could do, as the Committee of the Royal Yacht Squadron wished to give her a chance to compete against the pick of our fleet, they provided a special cup to be raced for.

The race for this cup, owing to mismanagement, did no such thing. The morning of the race the Squadron issued race cards and a programme; these cards, containing the names and colours of the yachts, described the course as being "round the Isle of Wight". The printed programmes stated that the race was to be "round the Isle of Wight outside the Nab". This led to a misunderstanding. *Volante, Arrow, Bacchante, Constance* and *Aurora* bore away and made for the Nab. The remaining yachts that were racing, among them the *America*, took the inside course. As the wind was from the west, the first five vessels named were greatly handicapped, as, in addition to the increased length of course, they came up to a windward position of the *America*, and *America* won the cup which has cost so much money to hold.

An item of interest in describing the race is recorded in *Bell's Life*. When the *America* passed the Royal Yacht *Victoria and Albert*, which was just inside the passage off Alum Bay, with Queen Victoria, the Prince Consort and the Prince of Wales, afterwards King Edward VII, aboard, the *America*, as is the custom at sea, lowered her ensign and, what is probably unique, the Commodore and the crew took off their caps and remained uncovered whilst passing the yacht.

Sixty Years of Yachts, Herbert E. Julyan, 1950

America's Cup

America, 1885

Stories of American Yachtsmen

As the English representative of the largest firm of naval architects in New York, I was brought into touch with some of America's most wealthy yachtsmen.

A friend one day said to Mr. J. P. Morgan, the American banker, after looking over the luxurious motor yacht *Corsair*:

"How much does it cost to run a yacht?"

"You cannot afford to run a yacht," replied Mr. Morgan.

"Why? I am pretty warm, you know."

"Yes," said Mr. Morgan, "but anyone who has to ask how much it costs to run a yacht cannot afford to keep one."

The first large yacht laid down was the *Valiant*, 2,184 tons, built by Laird Bros. for W. K. Vanderbilt. I never heard what she cost to build, but it must have been something like £150,000. We had her for sale about ten years after at £90,000.

Sixty Years of Yachts, Herbert E. Julyan, 1950

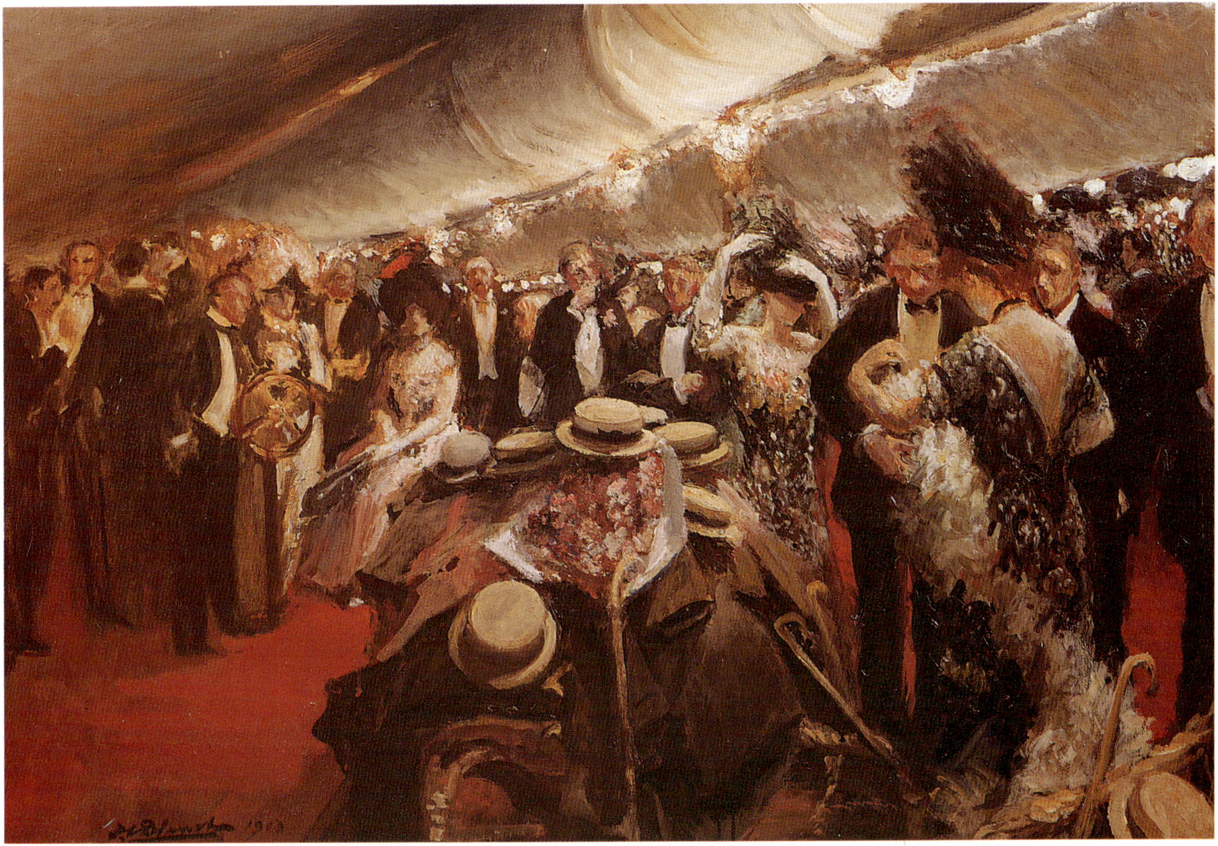

THE TRUE SEA

Already I looked with other eyes upon the sea. I knew it capable of betraying the generous ardour of youth as implacably as, indifferent to evil and good, it would have betrayed the basest greed or the noblest heroism. My conception of its magnanimous greatness was gone. And I looked upon the true sea – the sea that plays with men till their hearts are broken, and wears stout ships to death. Nothing can touch the brooding bitterness of its soul. Open to all and faithful to none, it exercises its fascination for the undoing of the best. To love it is not well. It knows no bond of plighted troth, no fidelity to misfortune, to long companionship, to long devotion. The promise it holds out perpetually is very great; but the only secret of its possession is strength, strength – the jealous, sleepless strength of a man guarding a coveted treasure within his gates.

The Mirror of the Sea, Joseph Conrad, 1906

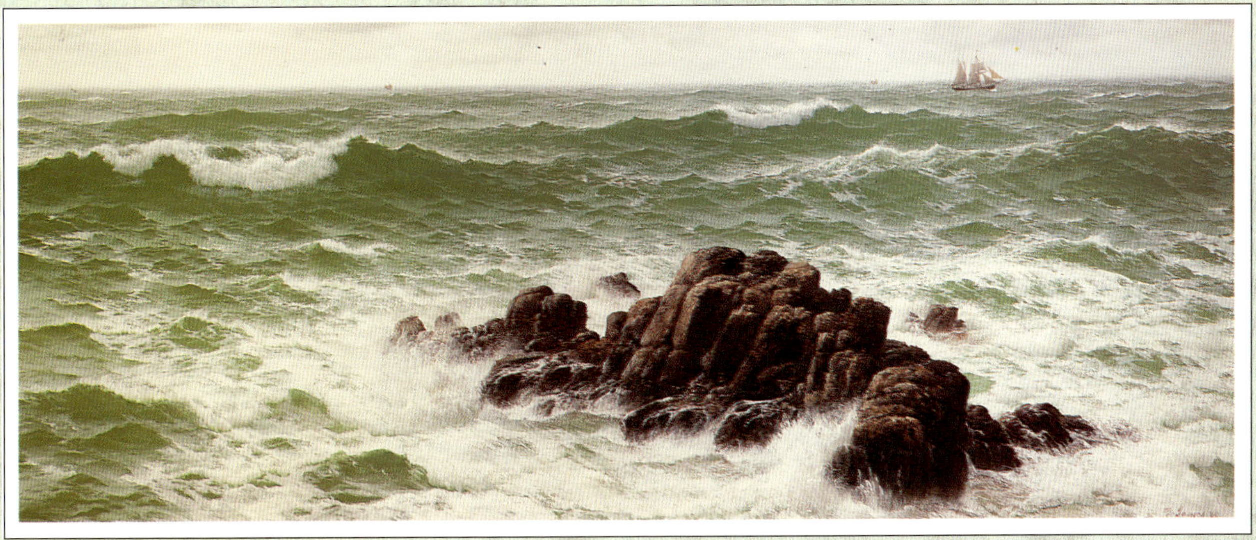

At The Helm and Overboard

'The big white cutter's rail was awash, sometimes under in the severe puffs. There was a nasty chop but not much sea, and the wind had piped up to about thirty miles an hour. I was at the wheel, and had asked John Christensen, *Yankee's* skipper, to stand by and help me gybe round the mark. As I yelled this to him against the whistle of the wind, I held *Yankee* off slightly, to cut the buoy as close as possible. Suddenly there was a grinding, crunching noise, such as I had never heard. Mystified, I lifted my eyes from the water and looked aloft. There in that second I saw *Yankee's* towering rig, 156 feet of it, steel mast, sails and gear, go crumpling and falling to leeward in one ghastly mass!

'In a flash it was over the side. Instinctively I dodged to windward as the main boom struck the deck, and clung to the wheel in an effort to keep the yacht under control. The sodden mainsail and the tough steel mast acted as a brake, and we swung to leeward and came immediately to a stop. Two men were thrown overboard, strangely enough, to windward. They were quickly recovered, and as our competitors sailed by we signalled that all was well.'

Sacred Cowes, Anthony Heckstall-Smith, 1965

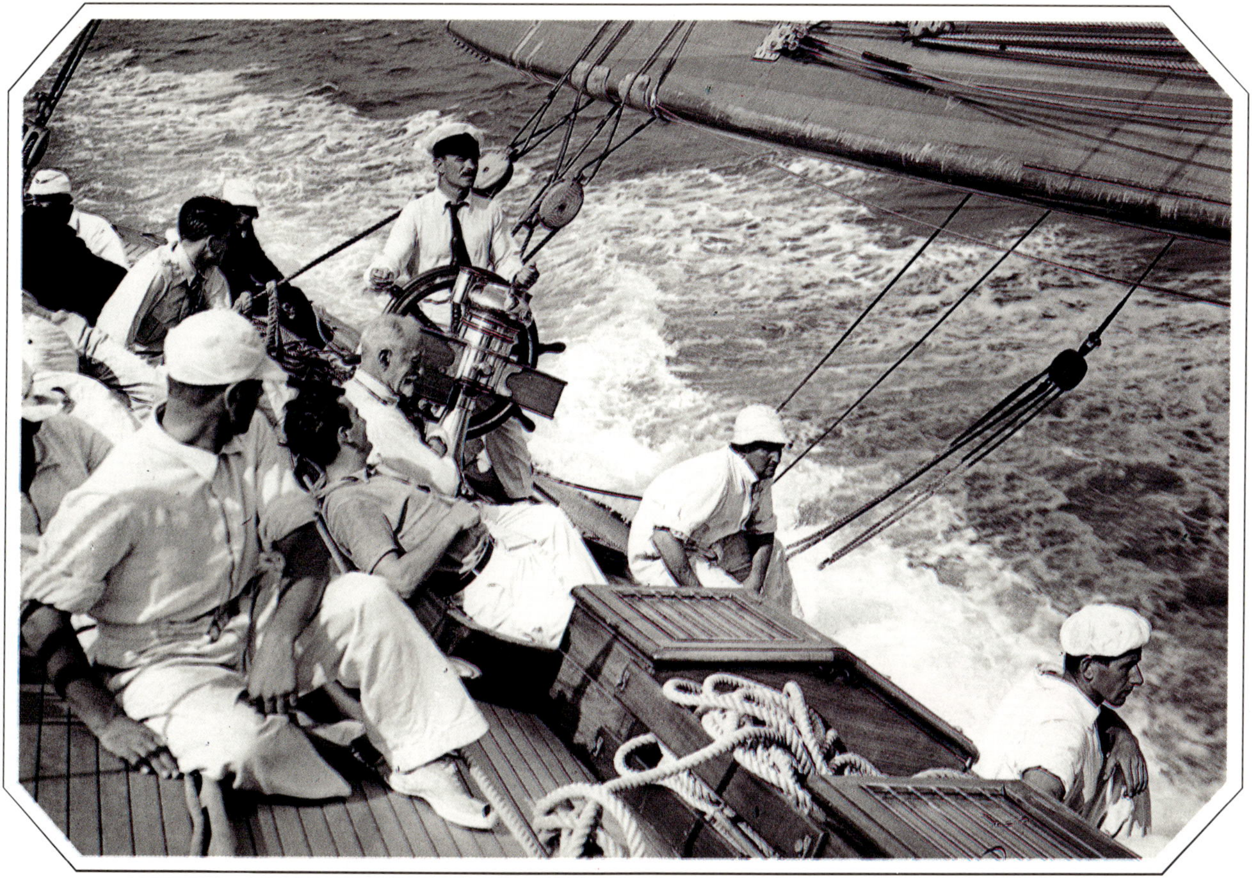

ADIEU, MY NATIVE SHORE

Adieu, adieu! my native shore
   Fades o'er the waters blue;
The night-winds sigh, the breakers roar,
   And shrieks the wild sea-mew.
Yon sun that sets upon the sea
   We follow in his flight;
Farewell awhile to him and thee,
   My native Land — Good night!

Childe Harold's Pilgrimage, Lord Byron, 1818

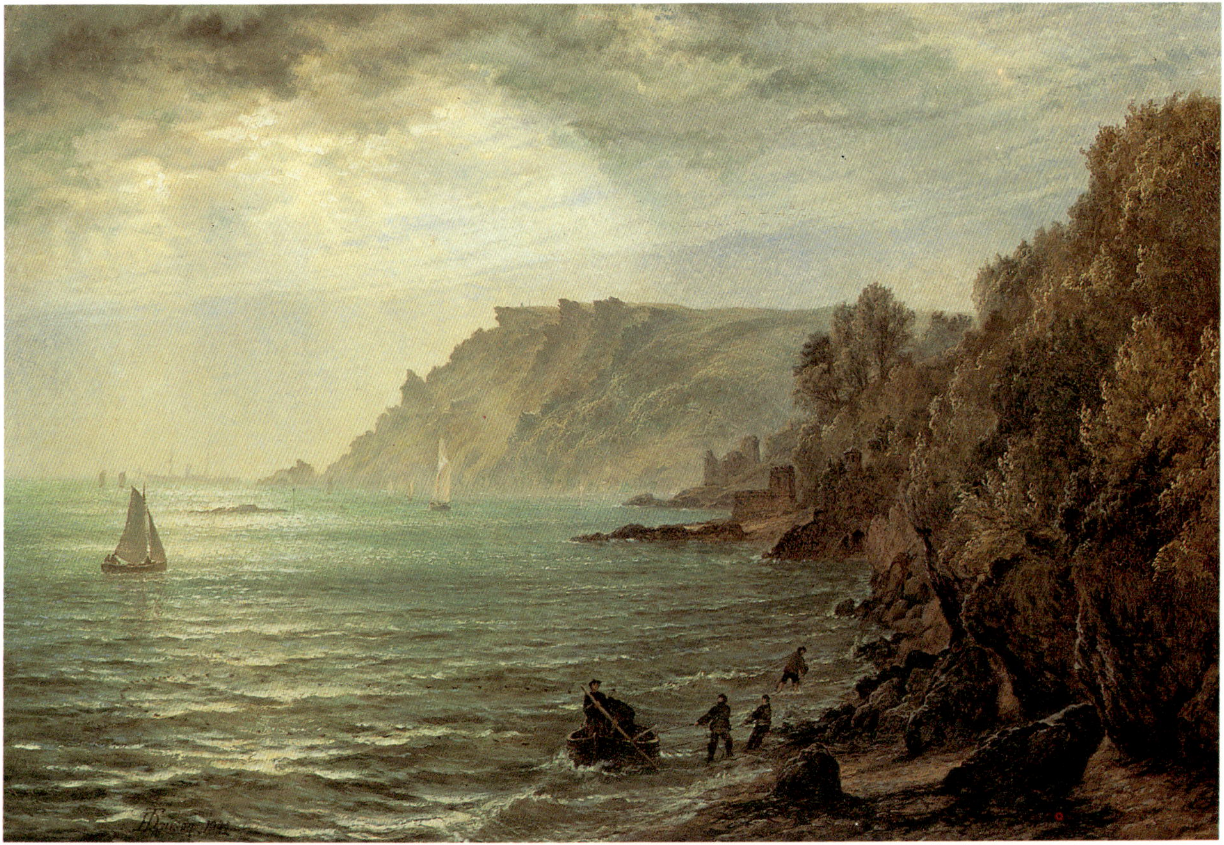

Acknowledgements

PICTURE CREDITS

Front cover: *Lee-Rail Awash*, Arthur Hopkins (Bridgeman Art Library/Atkinson Art Library, Southport, Lancs)
Title page: *H.M. Yacht 'Britannia' at Cowes, 1913*, N. Sotheby Pitcher (Bridgeman/Bonhams)

3 *On Board the Yacht 'Candida'* (Hulton Picture Company)
5 *The Bridge at Grez, 1883*, Sir John Lavery (Fine Art Society, London)
6 *Messing About in Boats*, Arthur Rackham (Mary Evans Picture Library)
7 *Boulter's Lock* (Hulton Picture Company)
9 *Boating on the River*, Jules Frederic Bellavoine (Bridgeman/Josef Mensing Gallery, Hamm-Rhynern)
10 *Mr Punch Goes Afloat* (Punch Picture Library)
11 *View of the Thames at Westminster Looking Towards Lambeth, 1818*, Jacques Laurent Agasse (Fondation Thyssen-Bornemisza, Lugano)
13 *Eights at Henley*, John Cosmo Clark (Bridgeman)
14 *Henley Regatta, 1906* (Hulton Picture Library)
15 *Henley Regatta*, James Tissot (Bridgeman/Private Collection)
16 *Henley Regatta, 1890* (Mary Evans Picture Library)
17 *A Victorian River Party, c. 1895* (Popperfoto)
18 *Henley* (Mary Evans Picture Library)
19 *At the Regatta*, Hector Caffieri (Fine Art Photographs)
21 *Boulter's Lock Sunday Afternoon, 1898*, Edward John Gregory (The Board of Trustees of the National Museums and Galleries on Merseyside, Lady Lever Art Gallery, Port Sunlight)
22 *The Fourth of June* (by permission of the Provost & Fellows of Eton College)
23 *The Fourth of June*, William Evans (by permission of the Provost & Fellows of Eton College)
25 *Hammersmith Bridge on Boat Race Day*, Walter Greaves (Tate Gallery)
27 *Regatta off Long Sand Lightship, 1886*, Anon (Bridgeman/Private Collection)
29 *'Undaunted' off Ailsa Craig, with Merchant Ships Beyond, 1871*, C.H. Fyfe (Bridgeman/Christie's, London)
31 *H.M. Yacht 'Victoria', 1880*, George Gregory (Bridgeman/Royal Thames Yacht Club, London)
33 *Schooner off the Edistone Lighthouse*, Nicholas Matthew Condy (Bridgeman/David Messum Fine Paintings)
34 *Yacht at Cowes, 1908* (Mary Evans Picture Library)
35 *Cowes with Royal yacht 'Britannia', July 1909* (Hulton Picture Company)
37 *The 'Aveyron' winning the Prince of Wales Challenge Cup*, John Moore (Fine Art Photographs)
39 *'Westward' 1911* (Beken of Cowes)
40 *'Sonya'* (Beken of Cowes)
41 *King Alfonso of Spain with King George V* (Beken of Cowes)
43 *King George V at the Wheel* (Beken of Cowes)
45 *'Britannia', 1924* (Beken of Cowes)
47 *'America'* (Beken of Cowes)
49 *Dinner on Board the Yacht 'Vanderbilt' at Cowes, 1909*, Jacques Emile Blanche (Robert Harding Picture Library/Rainbird Collection)
51 *Peel Rock, Land's End, Cornwall*, David James (Bridgeman/J. Collins & Son Fine Paintings, Devon)
52 *Tommy Sopwith on 'Endeavour'* (Hulton Picture Company)
53 *'Candida', 1935* (Hulton Picture Company)
55 *Salcombe Estuary*, Henry T. Dawson (Bridgeman/Royal Holloway College)

TEXT CREDITS

Text extracts for the following sources are reprinted with the kind permission of the publishers and copyright holders stated. Should any copyright holder have been inadvertently omitted they should apply to the publishers who will be pleased to credit them in any subsequent editions.

8 H.E. Bates, *The Feast of July* (Michael Joseph, 1954, The Estate of H.E. Bates)
12 Max Beerbohm, *Zuleika Dobson* (© Mrs. Eva Reichmann)
36, 38, 42, 44, 52: Anthony Heckstall-Smith, *Sacred Cowes* (Anthony Blond, 1965) 40, 46, 48: Herbert E. Julyan, *Sixty Years of Yachts* (Hutchinson, 1950)

First published in Great Britain 1991 for
ABERCROMBIE & FITCH, INC.
by Pavilion Books Limited
196 Shaftesbury Avenue, London WC2H 8JL

Anthology compilation and introduction text copyright © Jenny de Gex 1991
For other copyright holders see Acknowledgements.

Designed by Andrew Barron & Collis Clements Associates

All rights reserved. No part of this publication may be reproduced, stored in a retrieval system, or transmitted, in any form or by any means, electronic, mechanical, photocopying, recording or otherwise, without the prior permission of the copyright holder.

A CIP catalogue record for this book is available from the British Library

ISBN 1-85145-8425

Printed and bound in Scotland by Eagle Colour Books.